Airplanes

Kelli Hicks

rourkeeducationalmedia.com

Scan for Related Titles and Teacher Resources

Before & After Reading Activities

Teaching Focus:
Concepts of Print- Have students find capital letters and punctuation in a sentence. Ask students to explain the purpose for using them in a sentence.

Before Reading:

Building Academic Vocabulary and Background Knowledge
Before reading a book, it is important to set the stage for your child or student by using pre-reading strategies. This will help them develop their vocabulary, increase their reading comprehension, and make connections across the curriculum.
1. *Read the title and look at the cover. Let's make predictions about what this book will be about.*
2. *Take a picture walk by talking about the pictures/photographs in the book. Implant the vocabulary as you take the picture walk. Be sure to talk about the text features such as headings, the Table of Contents, glossary, bolded words, captions, charts/diagrams, or index.*
3. *Have students read the first page of text with you then have students read the remaining text.*
4. *Strategy Talk – use to assist students while reading.*
   - Get your mouth ready
   - Look at the picture
   - Think…does it make sense
   - Think…does it look right
   - Think…does it sound right
   - Chunk it – by looking for a part you know
5. *Read it again.*
6. *After reading the book complete the activities below.*

Content Area Vocabulary
Use glossary words in a sentence.

airfoil
air pressure
drag
overcomes
resistance
thrust

After Reading:

Comprehension and Extension Activity
After reading the book, work on the following questions with your child or students in order to check their level of reading comprehension and content mastery.
1. *What does thrust mean? (Summarize)*
2. *How have airplanes changed the way we travel? (Text to self connection)*
3. *How does the curved shape of a wing help the plane fly? (Asking questions)*
4. *What factors affect an airplane's ability to fly? (Summarize)*

Extension Activity
Create a paper airplane! Using a sheet of paper, fold it to create an airplane. Throw your plane and record how far it flew. Now make adjustments on the plane and throw it again. Did it fly farther? How did it fly? Record your observations. Continue to make adjustments and record your observations until you create the best paper airplane!

Table of Contents

Ready to Fly

Fasten your seat belt and get ready to take off.

Airplanes make traveling long distances quick and easy.

Each year 64 million planes take off in the United States. Can you imagine how many take off worldwide?

Today's airplanes are very large and heavy.

So how do they manage to get so high up in the air?

7

Air Force

Four factors affect an airplane's ability to fly: weight, lift, **thrust**, and **drag.**

Air flows over moving things such as cars and airplanes. Aerodynamics is the study of how that air moves.

air flow

Weight and drag work against an airplane. The weight of the airplane pulls the airplane down.

Air flows over the aircraft, which creates drag, or air **resistance.**

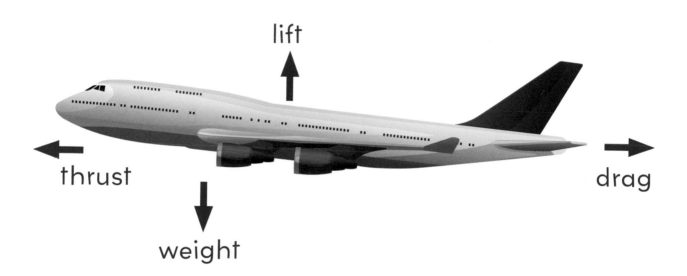

lift

thrust

drag

weight

Fighting the Drag

The curved shape of an airplane wing is called **airfoil.** It creates lift that fights gravity.

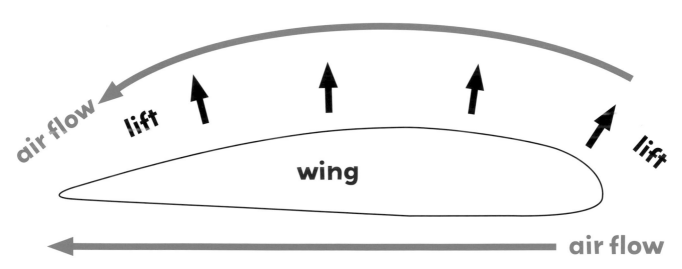

Air flows over and under the wing. Its curved shape forces the air flowing over the wing to move faster. The **air pressure** is low.

Air flowing under the wing moves slower causing higher air pressure. This causes lift. As the speed of the airplane increases, it rises off the ground.

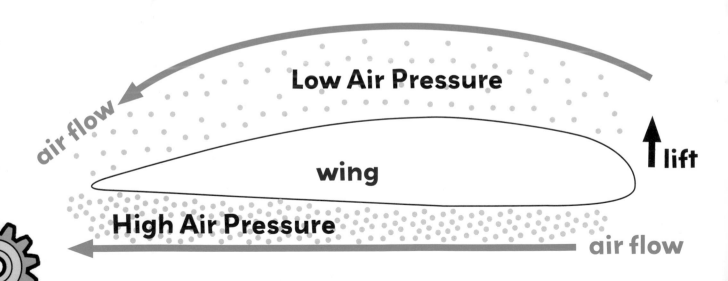

Low Air Pressure

air flow

lift

wing

High Air Pressure

air flow

Lift must be equal to or greater than the weight of the plane to keep it in the air.

lift

C→

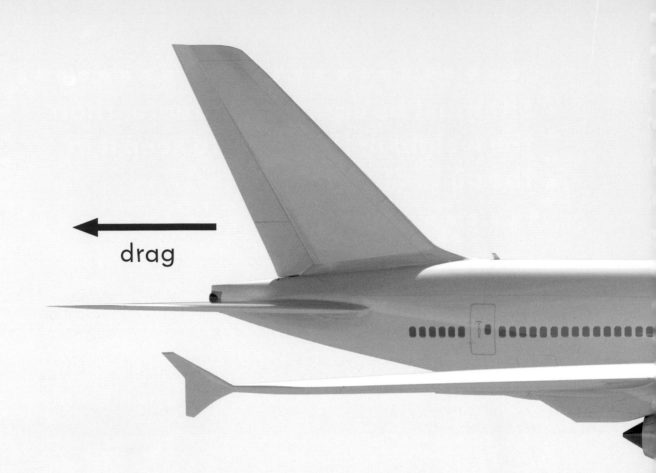

drag

Thrust is the opposite of drag. The force of a jet engine helps move the airplane forward. It **overcomes** the drag.

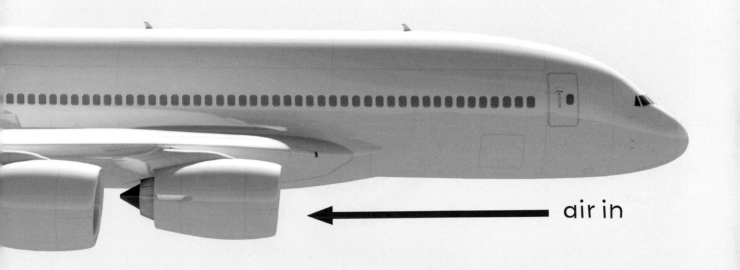

air in

Jet fuel heats the engine air. The hot air leaves the engine, with great force, or thrust.

Then the airplane moves forward, faster and faster. Soon it has lift off.

The pilot controls the airplane, steers it, and makes sure it heads to the correct destination.

Now, sit back, relax, and enjoy the flight!

21

Photo Glossary

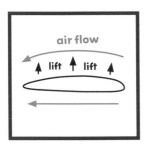

airfoil (air-FOIL): The curved shape of an airplane wing, which helps keep it in the air.

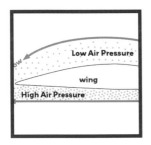

air pressure (air PRESH-ur): The force of air, which pushes down on something is called pressure.

drag (drag): Something that prevents or slows forward motion creates drag.

overcomes (oh-vur-KUHMZ): One overcomes a problem by defeating it or getting control of it.

resistance (ri-ZIS-tuhns): Resistance is the ability to fight off or overcome something.

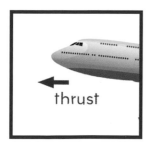

thrust (thruhst): The forward force created by a jet engine is called thrust.

Index

Websites to Visit

www.grc.nasa.gov/www/k-12/UEET/StudentSite/aeronautics.html

www.airplanesforkids.com/page/page/1292990.htm

www.sciencekids.co.nz/sciencefacts/flight.html

About the Author

Kelli Hicks is a teacher and author who lives in Tampa, Florida with her husband, two kids, and golden retriever. When she isn't writing or coaching soccer, she dreams about flying in an airplane to see her brothers, sister, nieces and nephews up north.

Meet The Author!
www.meetREMauthors.com

www.rourkeeducationalmedia.com

PHOTO CREDITS: Cover © Peter Guess; title page, 15 © strevens; page 4 © Blend Images; page 5, 23 © solarsteven; page 6, 23 © Sergey Plakhotin; page 9, 23 © 36clicks; page 11, 22 © omergenc; page 16 © cherezoff; 18 © tr3gin; page 19 © F. Schmidt; page 20 © andresrimaging; page 21 © Image Source;

Edited by: Jill Sherman

Cover by: Nicola Stratford, nicolastratford.com
Interior design by: Jen Thomas

Library of Congress PCN Data

Airplanes/ Kelli Hicks
(How It Works)
ISBN (hard cover)(alk. paper) 978-1-62717-649-1
ISBN (soft cover) 978-1-62717-771-9
ISBN (e-Book) 978-1-62717-891-4
Library of Congress Control Number: 2014934241

Printed in the United States of America, North Mankato, Minnesota

Also Available as:

ROURKE'S
e-Books